LOOKING

FOR T[...]LIGHT

A journey of pre[...]ing.

ASHLEIGH ASCOLI   POETRY & PROSE

Cover illustration by
Tanya Antusenok @tanita_arts

Internal illustrations by
Kseniia @xenipie and Subi @backyard_rose

For all those who are healing, grieving
and seeking out the light in the darkest of nights.

LOOKING FOR THE LIGHT

DEAR READER,

If this book has made its way into your hands, let me first say, I am sorry. I am sorry for the loss you have endured and the grief you now carry. I know how heavy it can feel, how exhausting it can be and how dark it can seem.

I am not an expert on grief, I am not an expert on miscarriage - but I have been where you are, I have felt what you feel and I am walking right alongside you.

I hope you find healing and hope within these pages. I hope the days are gentle and the nights are speckled with stars. I hope you find enough joy, no matter how small, to remind you that this life is beautiful.

I hope you find the light you are searching for, and that even in the darkest of nights, you remember that the sun will always rise.

With strength, love and healing.

Ash x

LOOKING FOR THE LIGHT

FOREWORD

This collection is divided into two sections:
The Darkest Night and *The Sun Will Rise.*

The Darkest Night is a series of poems for when you need to find solace in your grief, to know that you are not alone and that others have felt, and feel, the depth of your pain.

The Sun Will Rise is a series of poems and positive affirmations for when you need a gentle reminder that there are brighter days ahead, and though you will never forget your baby, your pain or your grief; there is light to be found, even in the darkest of nights.

THE DARKEST NIGHT

THE MAGIC NUMBER THREE

How many miscarriages?

We've had two now.

Well lucky it was early,

At least you weren't too attached,

And I can't run tests,

Unless you have more than that,

Three or more,

That's the golden ticket,

Two could be normal,

Three doesn't mean it isn't.

Just go home,

And get some rest,

Maybe try,

A little less stress.

If you have any more,
Then do come back,
Maybe I can run some tests,
After that.

How many miscarriages?

We've had five now,
And I'm really not sure,
If my body or mind,
Can take much more,
My soul is aching,
As my body bleeds,
Have I been through enough yet,
For you to help me?

BEASTS OF LOVE & LOSS

This grief often feels,

Like a gathering of beasts,

With snapping maws,

And tearing teeth,

They were born from love,

And carved from loss,

And I am but a scrap of meat,

To

     be

         torn

            apart

and tossed.

AM I SMALL ENOUGH YET?

On the days when the pain,

Sits like a stone in my stomach,

I find myself curling in,

With my knees to my chest;

As though I could become small enough,

For the grief to forget I exist.

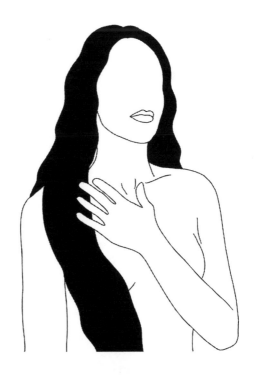

THE DARK

You were here and gone so quickly,

I could almost pretend,

That you were never even here,

To begin with;

But you left me empty,

A sky devoid of stars,

And there was no light left,

To guide me out of the dark.

BUZZING CICADAS

My nightmares are laced,

With the echo of pain,

Like buzzing cicadas,

That I can't escape:

A still ultrasound screen,

Fresh blood stains,

"I'm so sorry, there's no heartbeat,"

Repeated, again and again.

THE LOSS OF YOU

I did not stop loving you,

When I learned your heart,

Had ceased its beat;

But with nowhere for that love to go,

It built up in my tendons and bones,

So that every inch of my being,

Was weighed down and aching,

With the loss of you.

MY LONGING

Of all the empty places,

That exist within my soul,

I am most aware of those,

Which you used to call home,

They ache in your absence,

Demanding to be filled,

But nothing can satisfy,

My longing for you.

BE POSITIVE

How I wish,

You would stop,

Searching for silver linings,

In the clouds of my loss;

They are already heavy,

Weighed down with grief,

Please don't add to them,

With your 'be positive' and 'at least.'

TANGERINE SKIES

Fallen eyelashes,

The arc of a rainbow,

Delicate new blooms,

And the moon's silver glow.

The month of November,

Sweet lemon slice,

The number twenty-two,

And tangerine skies.

These are the things,

That remind me of you,

And all the breadth between them,

Is laced with you too.

FEROCITY

The strength with which we love,

Often determines,

The strength with which we grieve,

And with each aching loss,

It became easy to regret,

Loving with such ferocity,

And yet I could not help,

But carve out a place for you,

Within myself.

ALONE

My body feels an awfully lonely place,
Now that I'm the only one inhabiting it.

THE QUESTIONS I WHISPER INTO THE ABYSS

Why couldn't my love,

Strong and true as it was,

Keep you safely seeded,

Within my womb?

Why did the universe let me taste,

The sweet nectar of hope,

Only to turn it sour,

The moment it reached my throat?

Why did you bud just long enough,

To plant roots in my soul;

But never long enough

To thrive, bloom and grow?

Why are there so many questions,

That no one seems to have the answers to?

HOLLOW

There are days, moments and instances,

Where I am achingly aware,

Of the emptiness of my womb,

Where there should be kicks, flips and rolls,

There is an ever-growing hollow,

As though even my bones,

Recognise the loss,

And ache for you all the while.

ROT

I reached out,

Begging you to plant,

Healing words in my wounds,

But you dug me out deeper,

To plant your roots,

And you stepped back to watch,

As you left me to rot.

HEAVY

The irony of loss,

Is that I feel so heavy,

And weighed down,

By the absence of you.

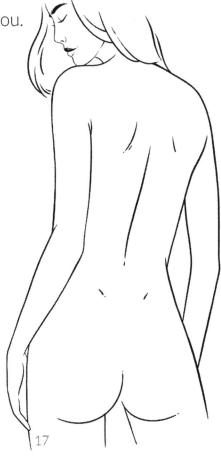

GRAVEYARD

Logically,

I knew I wasn't to blame,

But in the depths of my grief,

My womb felt like a place,

Healthy babies went to die,

My body felt like a graveyard,

And my faith felt like a lie.

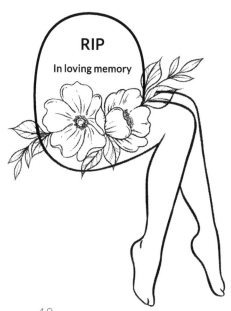

SUNLIGHT ON A SPIDER'S WEB

Today I saw the sunlight,

Sparkle on a spider's web,

And I stopped to marvel,

At the magic of it.

I reached out to touch it,

To try to catch the light,

But my hands were clumsy,

And it collapsed before my eyes.

That spider's web,

Is reminiscent of my healing -

The moment I stop to reach for it,

To examine it's existent,

It disintegrates in my hands,

As though it was never even there.

OUR ALTERNATE EXISTENCE

In an ever-expanding universe,

Of parallel realities,

I can only hope that somewhere,

There is a version of me,

That never lost you;

That never heard,

Those earth shattering words,

That never knew what it was,

To say *goodbye*,

Before we even had the chance,

To say *hello*.

FLAW

The fatal flaw of my heart,

Will surely be the ease with which,

I carve away parts of myself,

To create a place for you to fit.

DRIED PEONIES

I keep hold of old pregnancy tests,

Their colour slowly leaching,

Like dried peonies pressed,

In the pages of an old diary,

They're brittle with age,

Their beauty subdued,

But they remind me of days,

When my hope once bloomed.

MY GRIEF IS NOT A PLACE FOR SHAME

I do not have to apologise for:

Feeling my emotions,

Putting myself first,

Saying 'no' to things I know,

Will only make me feel worse.

Stopping to rest,

When the pain takes its toll,

Letting my tears fall,

To water my withered soul.

Giving myself time,

And the space I need,

To nurture my body,

And heal through my grief.

THE WEIGHT OF FAITH

I wish I could submerge myself,

Beneath the weight of another's faith,

To believe with such conviction and certainty,

That all would be okay;

But my hope has been tested,

And it's slipping through my teeth,

Because I know the cost that comes,

With blind belief.

PAPER THIN

You tried to create,

A refuge within me,

To build yourself a home,

Amongst my flesh, blood and bone,

But you were a flame,

And I was paper thin,

And we crumbled to ash,

Before we could even begin.

OVERRIPE FRUIT

When I say, *I'm doing okay,* what I really mean is:

There's an ache in my chest, where my heart once bloomed; before the flowers I planted there, were ripped out by the roots.

I mean, I'm trying to keep my head, above these raging waves; but honestly, I can barely open my eyes some days.

I mean, sometimes simply breathing, seems an impossible task. The air feels too heavy and it burns through my lungs.

I mean, my soul feels bruised, as overripe fruit, and I fear it's no longer sweet enough, for anyone to consume.

DROWNING

Grief often feels like I'm in the ocean,

With waves crashing overhead,

And I'm gasping,

And trying to catch a breath,

I can see you on the shoreline,

Smiling at me,

Because you're sure that I can swim,

But I can't catch my breath long enough,

To tell you that *I'm drowning.*

CONVERSING WITH THE STARS

I told the stars about you,

I whispered my love to the moon,

I begged the sun to keep you safe,

I asked the earth to help you bloom.

I wonder if they heard my pleas,

If they listened to my cries;

Or did they turn their heads away,

To avoid the pain in my eyes?

BURN

I thought I could ignore my grief,

And it would simply fizzle out,

But it was like trying to ignore a flame,

Only to look down and find,

That my skin was smoldering,

And I was being burnt alive.

THIS IS NOT YOUR FAULT

A drafted list of all the things,
I wish someone had told me:

This is not your fault.
You are allowed to grieve.
It's okay to wear your heart,
On the outside of your sleeve.
Your body is not the enemy.
This does not dictate your worth.
Running from the pain,
Will not ease the hurt.
You're allowed to take the time,
However long it may be,
To rise above these waves,
And find the calm in this sea.

I'M OKAY

I keep the words,

I'm okay,

Tucked between my teeth,

Whilst the truth,

That *I'm drowning,*

Is held tightly,

Against the insides of my cheeks.

SHADES OF PINK

My favourite shade of pink,

Is that which appears,

In a first positive pregnancy test;

When it's pale as the sky after sunrise,

But holds a lifetime of hope.

My least favourite shade of pink,

Is that which appears,

In the first drops of fresh blood,

When your heart is ripped from your chest,

And you're

     falling,

            falling,

                  falling,

Into the abyss.

BETWEEN THE NOTES

I see you,
Between the space,
Of dreaming and awake.

I hear you,
As I hum along,
To my favourite song.

I feel you,
Inside the breaths,
That ache through my chest.

MY WELL-REHEARSED LINE

When you ask what's on my mind, I think of the fact that I'm paper-thin, and there's a fire smoldering, mere inches from my being.

I think of the fact that there's a spider building her home, in the space between my breath and bones. She's spinning her web and laying her eggs, in the growing expanse of my emptiness.

I think of the fact that I've got a glass jar, tucked away in the confines of my heart. It's filled with memories and half-formed thoughts, that keep me awake into the dawn.

Yet the words that whisper past my lips, don't sound anything like this. Instead I smile, and bite my tongue, and whisper my well-rehearsed line, 'Nothing, I'm fine.'

MY SEARCH HISTORY

Can a loss be caused by stress,

Another word for grief,

Percentage decrease of miscarriage,

After hearing a heartbeat.

Easy self-care tips,

Parenting after loss,

Trying to conceive,

IVF options and costs.

Synonym for healing,

Antonym for lost,

Why, why, why,

Am I not good enough?

AN IVORY SILENCE

The cadence of your heartbeat,

An ivory silence,

The echoes of my screams,

Reverberate through the quiet;

This is our symphony,

The melody of grief,

And the thrum of loss,

Softly sings me to sleep.

ASHLEIGH ASCOLI

THE SUN WILL RISE

AFTER THE DARK

When the depths of this storm,

Pass overhead,

And the sun rises,

From her slumbering bed,

When the clouds depart,

And the thunder subsides,

When the lightning is no longer,

The only source of light,

Though you may feel weak,

You will rise,

Like the brightest star,

From the darkest night.

My body is beautiful
and worthy of love.

A SKYLIGHT FOR THE STARS

I was terrified of opening up,

Of showing you,

The darkest depths of my heart;

But you looked at my scars,

And the grief taking residence,

In my heart;

And you showed me,

That my broken parts,

Were but a skylight for the stars.

THE LOWS

Trust,

That the lows of life,

Are leading you,

To the undiscovered depths,

Of the universe,

Where untouched wonders,

And novel discoveries await.

I am worthy
of being a mother.

BREATHE OUT

If you're deep underwater,

With no sense of direction,

Breathe out,

The bubbles will lead you,

To the refuge of the surface;

And I think the same can be said of grief,

Breathe out,

Surrender,

Let go;

There is healing in simply giving in.

PHASES OF THE MOON

I'm not really okay,

But that's alright.

The moon continues to rise and fall,

With grace every night,

She does not falter,

Nor apologise,

For the times she's less than whole,

And neither shall I.

46

IN A BOTTLE

How I wish I could take your pain,

And send it in a bottle out to sea,

Watch it drift away with the current,

Until you feel the swell of sweet relief;

But grief can't be so easily lost,

It floats in with the sea foam,

You see grief is all the love you have,

Just longing for its home.

MY MOTHER

My mother does not garden,
Has never tended to a rose,
But she taught me a thing or two,
About the way a flower grows.

My mother always told me,
To seek and find the light,
That petals can still open,
Even in the darkest of nights.

My mother always told me,
That you do not get to choose,
The soil in which you're planted,
But even from sand beauty can bloom.

My mother always told me,
That every seed needs a little rain,
And even after a cyclone,
You can bud and rise again.

I can reach out for help.
I can seek support.
I can say 'no.'

THE SUN WILL RISE

When the night itself,

Is a living thing,

Pulsing with pain,

And aching with grief,

I close my eyes,

And hold my breath,

And cling tight to the hope,

That brighter days are ahead.

The sun will rise,

From the depths of this night,

And I will follow,

In her stride.

THRIVE

Plant soothing seeds of joy,

Within your aching wounds,

Tend to them daily,

From the petals to the roots,

And watch as you once again,

Thrive, flourish and bloom.

My grief is valid.
I am supported.
I am not alone.

THE SCENT OF LAVENDER

When healing drifts in,

Like the scent of lavender on the wind,

Do not shy away,

From her warm embrace.

It's okay to smile again,

It's okay to laugh,

It doesn't mean that you've forgotten,

Or that your grief has passed.

Joy and loss can co-exist,

In the garden of your heart,

Like the summer blooms of lavender,

Rising from your scars.

PEPPERMINT LEAVES

If healing had a perfume,

I think it would be that,

Of freshly mown grass,

And strongly brewed tea,

Salt spray from the ocean,

And torn peppermint leaves.

THE WARMTH OF HONEY

The sun whispers,

Her words honeyed with warmth,

Have hope my child -

You will survive this terrible storm.

WEATHERED & WORN

I have been weathered and worn,

By this grief and it's storm,

But I will rise,

Crinkled and torn,

Like the brightest star,

From the darkest dawn.

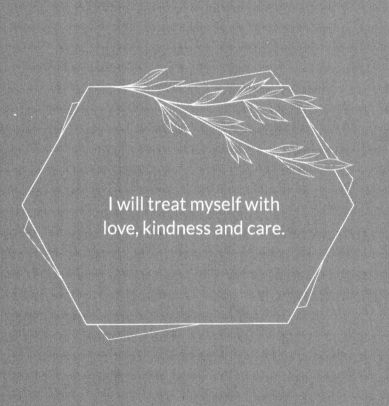

I will treat myself with
love, kindness and care.

THE MIRACULOUS & THE MUNDANE

Time is not,

The master magician,

It is but an ingredient,

In the healing potion,

Of time well-spent.

So dance barefoot,

Across a sandy plane,

Submerge your soul,

Beneath the salty sea waves.

Tip your face,

To the morning sun,

Drink heavily,

From the chalice of self-love.

Find joy and healing,

In the miraculous,

And the mundane,

Until you've filled with your world,

With so much light,

That the darkness,

Has to truly fight,

To make its way in.

My feelings are valid.
My feelings matter.

ECHO

I stood in the storm,

And danced in the rain,

As lightning leapt alongside me,

And the winds howled in vain,

I smiled through the downpour,

Of grief and pain,

And wept with joy,

As the thunder echoed your name.

GARDEN

When your heart stopped beating,

There was a gaping void in my chest,

That I didn't know how to fill.

At first I tried to hide its existence,

To cover it up and pretend it wasn't there,

But the more I ignored it,

The bigger it became.

So I filled that void,

With flowers and light,

And all that was good -

I planted a garden,

Where a graveyard once stood.

UNRAVEL

In a society where weakness,

Can be seen as a fault, flaw and failing,

It's important to have people and places,

Where you can safely unravel,

And be gently pieced back together.

OLD SCARS & NEW WOUNDS

Some days the hurt,

Will burst forth and bloom,

Tearing through old scars,

And opening new wounds.

On these days,

Use the space,

To rest,

To cry,

To breathe;

Be gentle with your healing heart,

It's doing it's best,

To mend these scars.

I welcome joy into my life,
even while I grieve.

SISTERS IN GRIEF

I found salvation,

In the refuge of your embrace,

You were a shelter from the rains,

A point of reference when I was lost,

A lighthouse to guide me,

Through the depths of this storm.

You were still mending,

Your own broken heart,

And yet you pulled back the curtains,

To let in the stars;

You showed me that despite,

My grief and pain,

I could still find the light,

And rise again.

For Amy Malan, thank you for holding space for my grief and leading me toward the light.

BURST FORTH & BLOOM

My grief felt so heavy,

That I was sure,

I had been buried alive,

Beneath the earth and soil;

But maybe I was simply a seed,

Planted exactly where I needed to be,

Waiting for the right time,

To burst forth, bloom and be set free.

THE CURE FOR GRIEF

Perhaps the cure for grief is a simple one:

Acknowledge it.

Lay down at the center of the cyclone,

And surrender to her chaos,

Close your eyes,

And let the storm rage through you.

REST YOUR WEARY LEGS

There will be days,

When the mere act,

Of shuffling your feet forward,

Will seem near impossible.

The fog of loss,

Will weigh down on you,

Too heavy to wade,

Your way through.

Give yourself permission,

To use these days,

To plant roots,

To tread water,

To rest your weary legs.

I am whole.
I am enough.
I am worthy.

ANEW

There was growth and transformation,

Amid the grief and pain,

As though the loss and heartache,

Had created greater space;

For wildflowers to bloom,

And the sun to shine through,

For the rains to trickle down,

And wash me anew.

SHINE

It is often those,

With aching hearts themselves,

That are first to reach out,

And pull back the veil;

To remind you that even,

In the darkest of nights,

The stars are still bright,

And the moon still shines.

METAMORPHOSIS

My grief was a chrysalis,
Of softly woven silk,
Until I resurfaced,
Wings pale as buttermilk;
A complete metamorphosis,
A shift from all I knew,
Neither better nor worse,
But transformed,
From loving you.

THE BETWEEN

I think I will always,

Exist in this place,

Between grieving my loss,

And entering healing's embrace.

COLOURLESS

This grief never really ends,

The pain will linger still,

But there are brighter days ahead;

Sweet as honey,

And soft as silk.

No, you won't forget,

And nothing will make your loss okay,

But the days won't always,

Be colourless and grey.

TIME LINE

You do not need to rush your grief,
There is no time line on healing.

Not all storms,
End with a sudden clear sky,
And a rainbow of hope.
Some fizzle out,
With a smattering of rain,
An occasional lightning strike,
Peaks of the sun through the clouds,
And the echo of thunder sighs.

RISE AND FALL

Let the sunset remind you,

That even the earth,

Must succumb to the dark,

Every now and then;

But there is beauty to be found,

In the rise and fall,

Of not only the sun,

But also you.

EBB AND FLOW

Just like the ocean's tide,

Your grief will ebb and flow,

Let the waves of loss take you,

Where they need you to go.

MY GRIEF DESERVES TENDERNESS

I am learning to be gentle,

And patient with my grief,

To not burn down a forest,

Because of a single withered leaf.

SIDE-BY-SIDE

There will be days,

When the healing and the hurt,

Sit side-by-side,

Like the crescent moon rising,

While the golden sun,

Is still high in the sky.

THE BIGGEST LIE I TOLD MYSELF

It will be easier,

If you just get up,

And wipe the tears from your eyes,

Hide behind a fake smile,

And pretend that you're alright;

The pain won't be able to hurt you,

If it can't catch you.

FINDING THE LIGHT

I fell,

Broke,

Healed,

And rose,

So I could be the mother and woman,

That my future children,

Could be proud of;

But somewhere along the way,

I looked for the light for myself as well,

Because even without my baby in my arms,

I know I am still worthy,

Of healing, rising and self-love.

LOOKING FOR THE LIGHT

ASHLEIGH ASCOLI

THANK YOU

There are many people I wish to thank. Many people who I owe a great deal of gratitude, for not only their support in this project, but for their love and care as I journey the rugged terrain of grief and pregnancy loss.

To my shelters in this storm, my points of reference when I am lost and my greatest gifts, Connor and Kyla. Thank you for loving me, even when I felt unworthy. Thank you for holding me, as I fell apart. Thank you for being patient, as I put myself back together.

I would like to thank my mother, who always helped me to see the stars, even in the darkest of nights. To my father, for showing me strength and courage. To my brother, for your care and eternal love. To my sister, who helped me pick up the pieces and rise on unsteady feet without ever letting me fall.

To the warrior women who came before me, and paved the way for my life; my grandmothers, Helen and Gillian and aunties, Simone and Debbie. To my grandfathers, Trevor and John. I am inspired by your strength, courage and love.

To Cody, thank you for always being in my corner, for inspiring me to be the best version of myself and for never tiring of my questions, brainstorming sessions and constant need for approval. No words will ever express my love and appreciation for you.

To Josie, thank you for being my safe place to unravel, for believing in me even when I didn't believe in myself and for always showing me the joy and beauty in life.

To Gabbie, thank you for loving and supporting me even when we were miles apart and your life was equally as busy. I am so thankful for you and miss you everyday.

To my amazing group of friends and family, who showed up for me and held space for my grief. Thank you for loving me, even when I felt hard to love. Thank you to Tammy, Kacey, Amy, Steph, Bree, Amy, Bridget, Rachel, Tamika, Hannah, Laura and Madi.

LOOKING FOR THE LIGHT

Printed in Great Britain
by Amazon

67135250R00056